FORENSIC
Investigations

LASTING IMPRESSIONS

Looking at Marks and Imprints

Leela Burnscott

Smart Apple Media

Smart Apple Media
P.O. Box 3263
Mankato, MN 56002

First published in 2009 by
MACMILLAN EDUCATION AUSTRALIA PTY LTD
15–19 Claremont Street, South Yarra 3141

Visit our website at www.macmillan.com.au or go directly to www.macmillanlibrary.com.au

Associated companies and representatives throughout the world.

Copyright © Leela Burnscott 2009

Library of Congress Cataloging-in-Publication Data

Burnscott, Leela.
    Lasting impressions: looking at marks and imprints / Leela Burnscott.
        p. cm. — (Forensic investigations)
    Includes index.
    ISBN 978-1-59920-460-4 (hardcover)
    1. Forensic sciences—Juvenile literature. 2. Evidence, Criminal—Juvenile literature. 3. Criminal investigation—Juvenile
    literature. 4. Crime scene searches—Juvenile literature. I. Title.
    HV8073.8.B867 2010
    363.25'62—dc22

                                                                    2009003448

Edited by Georgina Garner
Text and cover design by Cristina Neri, Canary Graphic Design
Page layout by Raul Diche
Photo research by Sarah Johnson
Illustrations by Alan Laver, Shelly Communications

Printed in the United States

Acknowledgments
The author and the publisher are grateful to the following for permission to reproduce copyright material:

Front cover photograph: Forensic evidence. Forensics officer dusting a wine bottle in order to reveal fingerprints left on the glass © Jim Varney, Science Photo Library/Photolibrary

Background images used throughout pages: fingerprint courtesy of iStockphoto/James Steidl; tweezers courtesy of iStockphoto/Mitar Holod; forensic investigation kit courtesy of iStockphoto/Brandon Alms.

Images courtesy of: © Department of Defence, **23**, **30** (top left and middle right); © R. J. Garrett, **21**; Getty Images/Dan Trevan/AFP, **4**; Getty Images/Todd Gipstein, **15**; Getty Images/Darde/AFP, **28**; *The Illustrated Guide to Forensics: True Crime Scene Investigations*, by Zakaria Erzinclioglu, **10**; iStockphoto/Alex Potemkin, **16** (right); iStockphoto/Anja Jerin, **5**; iStockphoto/Corey Sundahl, **29**; iStockphoto/Craig DeBourbon SSG C. A. DeBourbon, **22**; iStockphoto/Daniel Cooper, **11** (bottom); iStockphoto/Diane White Rosier, **24**; iStockphoto/Eric Renard, **18**; iStockphoto/George Clerk, **16** (middle); iStockphoto/Greg Nicholas, **30** (middle left); iStockphoto/Judith Bicking, **27**; iStockphoto/Robert Robinson, **17**; iStockphoto/Steve Mann, **16** (left); From RJ Johansen and CM Bowers, "Digital Analysis of Bitemark Evidence, 2002, published by Forensic Imaging Institute, Santa Barbara, CA, **13**; Photo Researchers/Photolibrary, **12**; Hubert Raguet/Eurelois/Science Photo Library/Photolibrary, **20**; Jim Varney/Science Photo Library/Photolibrary, **14**; Philippe Psaila/Science Photo Library/Photolibrary, **7**; Shutterstock/Kevin L Chesson, **6** (all); Shutterstock/Michael Ledray, **19**; Shutterstock/Perov Stanislav, **11** (top); Image copyright © Tyler Police Department, City of Tyler, Texas, **8**, **9**; Image copyright © Victorian Institute of Forensic Medicine, **26**, **30** (top right).

Text reference: Hugh Miller (1991). *Indelible Evidence: An International Collection of True Crimes which have been Solved by Forensic Science*, Crows Nest, NSW, Australia: ABC Enterprises, **28–9** (background information)

While every care has been taken to trace and acknowledge copyright, the publisher tenders their apologies for any accidental infringement where copyright has proved untraceable. Where the attempt has been unsuccessful, the publisher welcomes information that would redress the situation.

Contents

GLOSSARY WORDS

When a word is printed in **bold**, you can look up its meaning in the Glossary on page 31.

Science in the Court!

Forensic science is the use of scientific knowledge and techniques within the legal system, particularly in the investigation of crime. Forensic science can:

- determine if an **incident** resulted from an accident, natural causes, or a criminal act
- identify those involved in the incident
- identify and find those people responsible for the incident
- make sure that the innocent are not wrongly convicted

The term "forensic science" is quite misleading because it suggests only one type of science is involved. This is certainly not the case. Forensic investigations can involve virtually every field of science and technology, from electronics to psychology.

Forensic investigations require the skills of specially trained police, scientists, doctors, engineers, and other professionals. These investigators examine all types of evidence, from bloodstains to weapons and from bugs to computers. The greater the pool of evidence against an accused person, the greater the chance of a conviction.

A forensic expert presents crime scene photographs during a trial.

A shoe print can be used to identify the type of shoe worn by someone involved in an incident.

DID YOU KNOW?

A mark, such as a skid mark, is a noticeable **impression** left on top of a surface. An imprint, such as a footprint, is an impression pressed into a softer surface. A print, such as a fingerprint, may be either an imprint or a mark left on a surface.

Lasting Impressions

In the eyes of a forensic investigator, good impressions are very important. Impressions, such as fingerprints, are some of the most valuable pieces of evidence in a forensic investigation. They can link people to a crime scene or crime as well as provide information on any weapons used.

Luckily for forensic investigators, almost any object can leave behind a mark, imprint, or print. Each type of impression requires different specialized skills, training, and techniques to analyze it properly.

Fingerprints

Each person's fingers are covered in skin that has a unique pattern of ridges and grooves. Oil and sweat are constantly released through **pores** in the skin. This oil and sweat can produce a fingerprint, which is a copy of the skin pattern, when a finger makes contact with an object. Clear, well-formed fingerprints are often found on smooth, damp, or dusty surfaces.

Ridge Characteristics

Ridge patterns can be divided into three broad groups: whorls, loops, and arches. What makes each fingerprint unique are the individual ridge characteristics, called minutiae, within each of these groups. Minutiae include differences in ridge length and spacing. No two individuals have been found to have the same arrangements of minutiae.

Whorl fingerprint

Loop fingerprint

Arch fingerprint

DID YOU KNOW?

The American FBI's Integrated Automated Fingerprint Identification System contains fingerprint records for more than 55 million people, including those from convicted criminals and fingerprinted police officers.

Latent prints on a car license plate and CD are uncovered by spraying chemical glue on them.

Latent Fingerprints

Many fingerprints left behind at a crime scene are invisible to the naked eye. These latent prints can be made visible using special powders or chemicals.

Powders are generally used for prints on hard, non-absorbent surfaces such as glass. The surface is brushed lightly with a small amount of powder. The powder sticks to the oils left by the finger and reveals the fingerprint.

Chemicals are used on soft or absorbent surfaces such as paper. Some chemicals cannot be used at a crime scene because they are poisonous or dangerous. In these cases, objects from the crime scene are brought into a laboratory and treated with chemicals in specially designed cabinets. Some need to be placed under special light or heat before they reveal a fingerprint.

Many fingerprints are often found, but most are only smudges or partial prints. Only mostly or fully formed prints are useful for forensic investigations.

A police officer dusts a small object for latent prints in a laboratory.

Collecting Fingerprints

All fingerprints that are discovered must be immediately photographed. This is done:

- to provide a visual record of the fingerprint at the scene
- as a backup in case the print is accidentally lost, damaged, or destroyed
- so the fingerprint can be presented in court, if needed

Where possible, prints are collected from the scene for analysis in a laboratory. Small, movable objects are covered in cellophane or other suitable coverings to protect the print and are taken away.

Objects that are large or cannot be moved must have the prints "lifted" at the scene. Lifting prints involves covering the powdered fingerprint with a clear sticky material such as adhesive tape. The tape "lifts" the powder, transferring the print to the tape and producing a copy. The tape is then stuck to a special card. If not done carefully, the original print can be damaged or destroyed.

Analyzing Fingerprints

Forensic fingerprint analysis is always done by eye. In the past, investigators would take weeks to compare thousands of prints on record with a fingerprint from a crime scene. Today, computer programs search fingerprint **databases** and select the most likely matches. The investigator then examines each print by eye. Computers can identify over 100 possible matches, so it is still a very time-consuming job.

Two prints are classed as matching if somewhere between 8 to 16 points of similarity are found by at least two separate investigators. The number of points necessary for a match varies between countries.

DID YOU KNOW?

America's Automated Fingerprint Identification System (NAFIS) was launched in 1999. It is the largest computerized database of fingerprints in the world.

A forensic investigator compares a fingerprint match on a computer.

Other Body Prints

Almost any part of the body can leave behind a print. Only a few types, however, have been used in forensic investigations.

Ear Prints

Since the 1800s, there have been those who believe that each person has uniquely shaped ears. It has only been in the last 20 years or so that forensic ear-print identification has been used. It is a very new and controversial forensic science. Ear-print evidence is not widely used or accepted.

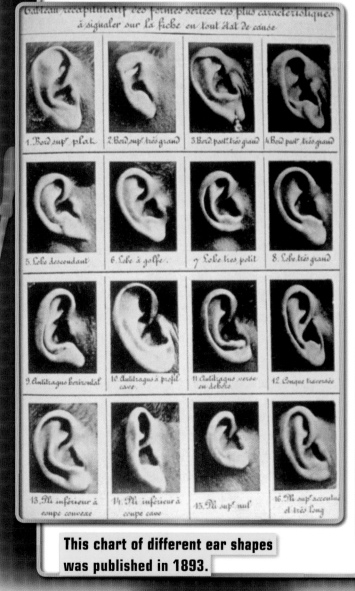

This chart of different ear shapes was published in 1893.

Just like with fingerprints, oils and sweat from an ear leave an outline when an ear is pressed on smooth surfaces. This can happen when someone presses their ear against a door or window to listen.

Ear-print evidence has only been used in a handful of court cases worldwide. Most times the evidence was disallowed or the case was thrown out on appeal.

CASE NOTE

In 1998, Britain became the first country to prosecute a person based on ear-print evidence. In 2004, however, a DNA sample recovered from the print proved that it was not the convicted man's ear print after all, and he was freed.

Footprints and Handprints

Identification based on bare footprints and handprints is a widely used forensic tool. These prints can help identify individuals based on:

- unique ridge patterns on the toes, sole, heel, and palm
- weight-bearing patterns, which occur because people put different pressure on different parts of their feet as they walk
- the shape and size of the prints

When footprints or handprints are left in soft materials such as soil, a cast can be made. This cast can be used for direct comparison with a suspect's foot or hand. If the suspect's foot or hand does not match the cast, then they could not have made the print. The size and shape of hands and feet differ according to a person's age, height, and weight. The prints of a child, a basketball player, and a sumo wrestler would all be very different.

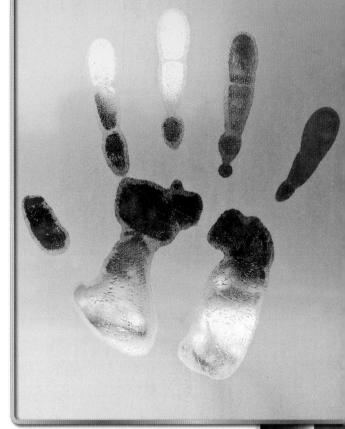

A handprint left at a crime scene can be used for direct comparison with a victim's or suspect's hand.

A footprint left at a crime scene can give information about a person's age, height, and weight.

Bite Marks

Bite marks can provide a great deal of information. Investigators have their work cut out for them, however, when a bitten object is badly damaged or decomposed. Sometimes, the bite marks of animals can look like other sorts of damage.

Types of Bite Marks

There are two main types of bite marks: complete marks and partial marks. Complete marks occur when both the upper and lower sets of teeth make firm contact. On skin, bleeding or bruising at the bite site often produces a clear impression of the biter's teeth.

Partial bite marks occur when:

- only the top or the bottom set of teeth bites down hard enough
- part of the evidence is bitten out, often only leaving the upper teeth pattern
- the bitten object is badly decomposed or damaged.

A bite mark is an impression of the biter's teeth.

A bite mark can provide a great deal of information, such as the distance between different pairs of teeth.

Analyzing Bite Marks

Every person has a unique set of teeth, which means that their bite marks should also be unique. Bite mark analysis can reveal the following features:

- the distance between different pairs of teeth
- the shape of the mouth's arch
- tooth alignment
- the width and thickness of teeth
- the spacing between teeth
- where any teeth are missing
- the curves of biting edges
- unique dentistry, such as metal crowns
- wear patterns, such as chips or ground-down teeth

CASE NOTE

Forensic dentists may be able to determine a person's physical appearance from a bite mark. Dental abnormalities, such as an overbite and overlapping teeth, may be due to a genetic condition that also causes a long thin face, a long nose, and breathing problems.

These features are compared to a suspect's teeth or their dental records to see if there is a match. Bite mark evidence is used to include or rule out suspects and is usually used alongside other evidence.

Shoe Prints

Shoe prints, like footprints, can be very useful forensic tools. Thousands of people can own the same type of shoe in the same size, however, so shoe prints are not unique.

Shoe Types

Most shoes these days have a distinct pattern on their sole. Some shoes even have a brand name on their soles. This makes each type of shoe highly identifiable.

Forensic investigators have used these sole patterns to their advantage. They have scanned the soles of thousands of different shoes into databases. This means a shoe print at a crime scene can be quickly identified. Police then know to check if anyone linked to the crime has that type of shoe.

Just owning a pair of shoes of the same make as those that left a print at a crime scene is not enough to convict someone. More matching details, such as wear patterns and contaminants, are required.

A plaster cast of a shoe print shows a distinctive pattern on the sole.

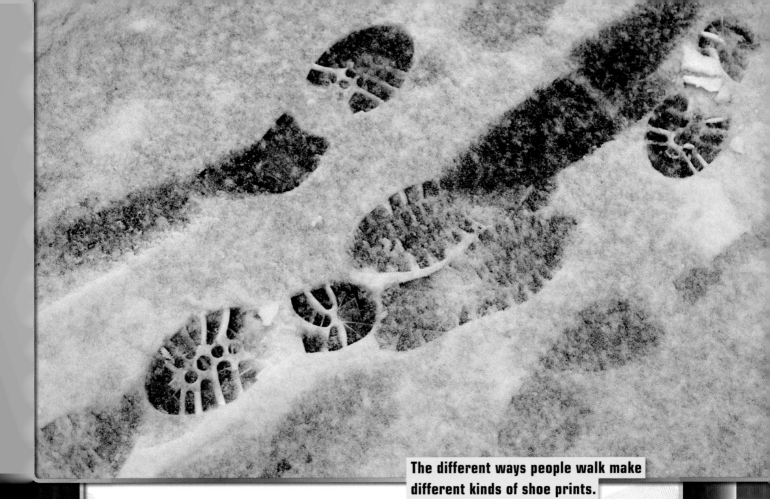

Wear Patterns

People wear out different parts of their shoes at different rates. For some people, it is always the outer heel that goes first, while for others it may be the sole under their big toe. This is because people's foot shape and weight distribution as they walk are different.

Wear patterns combined with sole patterns makes shoe print evidence a much stronger identification tool. It is highly unlikely that two people who own the same type of shoes in the same size will wear them out in exactly the same way.

Contaminants

Dirt, stones, plant matter, blood, and other materials can get trapped in the soles of shoes. These contaminants can be useful for two reasons. Firstly, they can produce easily identifiable marks on the shoe prints. Secondly, the material can be recovered from the shoe print or the shoe for analysis. This can help determine where the shoes were worn, further linking them to the crime scene.

Tire Impressions

Tires, like shoes, can leave identifiable impressions. Analysis of these impressions can involve two very different processes. The first process is studying individual tire marks to discover the vehicle that made them. The second process is analyzing skid marks left by tires to work out speed and other details.

Tire Markings

Car tires are similar to the soles of shoes in that nearly all brands have a unique **tread**. When tire impressions are left in soft surfaces, casts can be made for finer examination.

When analyzing tire impressions, forensic investigators measure or look for:

- the size or width of the tire
- the number of tires in the set of marks
- tread patterns
- wear patterns

A new tire has no wear patterns.

A tire this large is usually found on agricultural vehicles such as tractors.

A tire with this unique tread pattern would leave a distinct tire impression.

Analyzing Tire Impressions

The width of a tire impression is used to quickly determine if a bicycle, motorbike, car, or other vehicle was involved.

The number of tires in the set gives a clue as to the type of vehicle that made the marks. A single set of four prints indicates that either a car or small truck was present. Multiple sets of prints indicate that two or more vehicles were present. A single set of more than four tyre prints means that a truck was probably present. Generally, only trucks and articulated buses, also called "bendy buses," have more than four tires.

Tread pattern analysis can help pin down the exact type of vehicle. In many cases, certain tires fit only certain vehicles.

Wear patterns help track down the individual vehicle involved. Just like with shoe prints, investigators can compare wear marks on a tire print to suspect tires to find a match.

The width of these tire impressions suggests that a heavy vehicle such as a truck or tractor made them.

Skid Marks

Skid marks occur when a driver applies the brakes quickly. This causes the tires to scrape on the road, leaving behind some of the tire rubber. Skid marks are often critical pieces of evidence in hit-and-run incidents, single-vehicle or multi-vehicle accidents, and accidents involving pedestrians.

Crash investigators study the length, width, and direction of each skid mark to determine:

- the type of vehicle that made the marks
- the speed the vehicle was travelling
- where the vehicle began to brake
- if the vehicle swerved or was forced off the road
- if the vehicle was driving on the wrong side of the road

CASE NOTE

Finding no skid marks at a scene can be useful, too. The absence of skid marks can mean that the vehicle did not brake at all becaus

- the driver deliberately made impact and kept driving
- the driver did not notice that th had hit someone or something and drove on.

A driver may not notice they hit something if they are drunk or drugged. Also, drivers of large trucks may not feel the impact.

Skid marks last on the road surface for a long time, so they can be useful forensic tools long after the incident.

Officers analyze and measure skid marks at the scene of an accident.

Length and Position of Skid Marks

Short, sharp skid marks suggest that a vehicle was traveling at a reasonable speed. Long skid marks indicate high speeds. This is because the faster a vehicle is traveling, the longer it takes to come to a complete stop.

The position of skid marks can be important, too. In a pedestrian hit-run accident, skid marks found before the point of impact indicate that the driver saw the person and tried to stop. Skid marks found only after the point of impact indicate that the driver did not notice the person until they had hit them or that they deliberately ran them down and then braked.

Tool Marks

Tools and the marks they leave behind can be as individual as fingerprints. This is because the edges of all tools are thought to have unique **imperfections**. Some imperfections are visible to the naked eye, but most are only visible under a microscope.

Impressions on Tools

When tools are made, whether by hand or machine, they are left with a microscopic pattern of **striations** on their edges. These striations are produced as the tool is cut, finished, and sharpened.

Each time it is used, some of the tool is damaged or worn away. Over time, a unique wear pattern evolves. This wear pattern can include **macroscopic** or microscopic dents and chips on the tool's edge. Tools wear more when used on hard or rough surfaces.

A forensic investigator examines a tool for wear patterns and trace evidence.

Impressions Made by Tools

When tools are used with force on a surface, they leave an impression of their striations on the surface. The softer the surface, the greater the impression left by the tool.

The most common marks left behind by tools are:

- indentations in an object, from the tool being used with force
- **abrasions**, from the tool cutting or sliding against another object

Generally, the first thing a tool mark reveals is the type of tool used. By the size and shape of the mark, investigators can often quickly identify if the tool was a crowbar, screwdriver, chisel, or knife.

Matching Tools and Marks

Matching a specific tool to a mark can be quite difficult. Laboratory tests are often carried out with the suspect tool to try to reproduce the marks found at the crime scene. Photographs or casts of the test marks and the crime scene marks are compared. These tests do have a major drawback: the tool's original pattern may be damaged during the process.

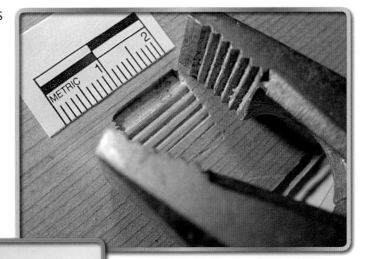

A pair of pliers is measured against an indentation made by a tool.

CASE NOTE

Tools are often used in burglaries and in crimes where forced entry is needed. Tool marks or impressions are often found at these types of crime scenes.

Firearm Markings

The way guns are manufactured creates a unique set of striations inside each gun barrel and on each firing mechanism. These striations mark the bullet during firing. Bullets are small parcels of gunpowder packed into a metal casing called a cartridge case or shell.

Cartridge Cases

When a gun's trigger is pulled, it creates a mini-explosion or a quick release of pressure or force. This normally causes the bullet and cartridge case to separate. The cartridge jumps backwards, hitting hard against the firing and loading mechanisms. This impact produces a perfect impression on the cartridge case.

Spent cartridges are ejected automatically from most guns. Once a suspect gun is found, investigators test-fire the gun and compare its marked cartridges to those found at the crime scene.

Bullets are surrounded by metal casings called cartridge cases.

A forensic expert uses a special microscope to compare markings on two bullets.

CASE NOTE

Different guns use different types of bullets. Bullets can vary greatly in size, shape, and weight. Bullet evidence helps experts narrow down what type of gun was used.

Bullets

When a gun is fired, the bullet is forced forward at high speed. As the bullet travels along the barrel, an impression of the barrel's striation pattern cuts into its surface. Each bullet fired by the same gun receives the exact same set of markings.

Since no two gun barrels have identical markings, no two guns will produce identically marked bullets. Test-firing a suspect gun will produce bullets for comparison with those used in a crime. This comparison cannot be done by the naked eye. **Ballistics experts** look at the bullets and cartridge cases under a special microscope.

Bruising and Livor Mortis

Bruising is caused by blood leaking out of damaged blood vessels and pooling under the skin. When a person dies, their blood settles naturally at the body's lowest points. This produces red–blue patches on the skin similar to bruising, called livor mortis or lividity.

By studying bruise and lividity patterns, **forensic pathologists** can discover:
- if a victim was moved after death
- if injuries were inflicted **ante-mortem** or **post-mortem**
- what caused any bruises on the body

Livor Mortis

Livor mortis can help a pathologist determine if a body was moved after death. A person left lying on their back for at least three hours after death will develop livor mortis along the back of their body. If the same body is found on its side, the pathologist will know that the body was moved because the livor mortis pattern will not match its position.

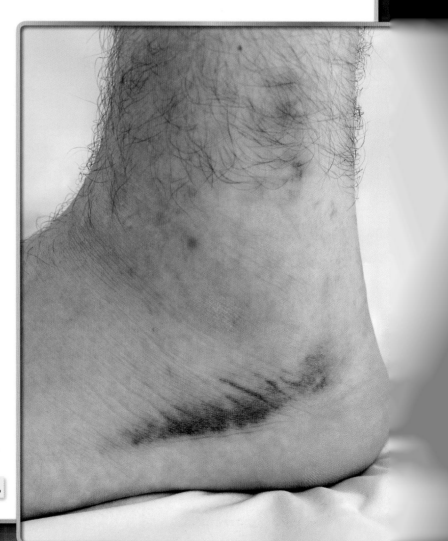

An injury causes a bruise if blood from damaged blood vessels pools under the skin.

ME SCENE—DO NOT CROSS—CRIME SC

Bruising

Most bruises start off pale, gradually turn "black and blue" and then after a few days turn yellow–brown and slowly fade away. The colour of a bruise can provide a rough estimate of when an injury occurred. It cannot, however, provide an exact time because bruising varies from person to person.

Bruises often take the shape of the object that caused the injury. This helps pathologists determine what caused the bruise, such as a fist or crowbar.

Under the Microscope

When a blood vessel is broken, the body releases natural **clotting factors** to "plug up" the hole. Once a person dies, no more clotting factors are produced so bleeding continues.

Pathologists can determine if a bruise occurred ante-mortem or post-mortem. If unclotted blood flows when the skin above the bruise is cut, then the bruise was the result of post-mortem injuries. If only clotted blood is found, then it was an ante-mortem injury.

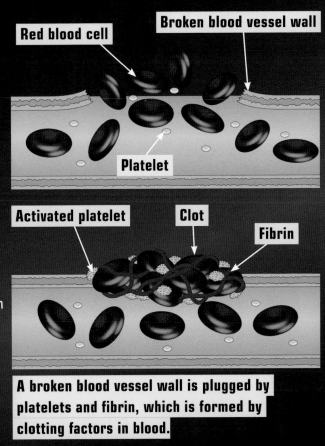

Red blood cell

Broken blood vessel wall

Platelet

Activated platelet

Clot

Fibrin

A broken blood vessel wall is plugged by platelets and fibrin, which is formed by clotting factors in blood.

To tell the difference between bruising and livor mortis, a pathologist presses down on the discoloured area. If a lighter patch occurs, it is a sign of livor mortis, because the blood is pushed away. Pressing against the broken vessels of a bruise does not change the colour of the bruise at all.

Other Marks

Forensic investigators can analyze other types of marks and impressions to help solve a case.

Jewelry Marks

Jewelry can leave pressure marks, tan marks, bruises, or grazes on skin. Pressure marks are most commonly caused by wearing rings and bracelets that are too small. When the jewelry is removed, an imprint is left on the skin.

Tan marks are most commonly caused by watches, but also by thick bracelets and necklaces. When someone is out in the sun, their skin that is exposed to the sun gets darker. The skin under the jewelry does not get darker. When their jewelry is removed, a lighter patch in the shape of the piece of jewelry can be seen.

Bruises and grazes occur when jewelry is forcefully removed from someone.

A tight wedding ring leaves a pressure mark on a finger when the ring is removed.

CASE NOTE

Finding jewelry marks on a murder victim but no jewel can suggest that robbery the **motive** for the crime. Finding the matching jewel the offender's possession them to the crime.

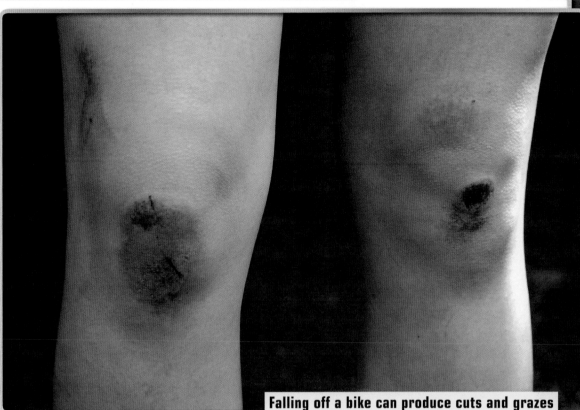

Falling off a bike can produce cuts and grazes from the scraping of skin along the road.

Cuts and Grazes

Cuts and grazes occur when skin is scraped along a surface, such as along the gravel of a road. Cuts and grazes on a victim can help investigators work out how, where, and with what a victim was injured. Cuts and grazes found on a victim lying in grass along the side of a road suggests that the victim made contact with the road. This could indicate a hit-and-run accident.

Dust and Fade Marks

Examining dust patterns and fade marks on the surface of furniture or on walls can occasionally be useful. This could help discover if something was stolen or moved from a room. An unfaded patch of wallpaper indicates that a picture or painting is missing. A round clear patch on a dusty shelf could indicate that a vase is missing. The missing object, such as the vase, could turn out to be the weapon that was used.

Murders in Northern Ireland

Background

From the late 1960s to late 1990s, the Provisional Irish Republican Army (PIRA) fought to free Northern Ireland from British rule. Over 1,000 people were murdered, including members of the Ulster Defence Regiment (UDR), a regiment of the British army.

The Crimes

A part-time member of the UDR was gunned down in his driveway south of Belfast, Northern Ireland. His son was shot dead while trying to help him. A few months later, police were called to a break-in in the same area. On arrival, three police officers were fatally gunned down.

The local three-man PIRA unit was suspected of both crimes. The identities of these men were already known to police. The police would later discover that another local had joined the unit. He had murdered the father and son and was involved in the murders of the police officers.

The murders occurred in Northern Ireland during a time of great conflict.

Bite marks on an apple were vital evidence in the case.

The Evidence

Bullets and cartridge cases were discovered at both crime scenes. Ballistics experts determined that these came from one gun.

A bitten apple was found at the first crime scene, near the place from where the gunman had fired. The apple was sent to the London School of Dentistry to be examined by a professor of **orthodontics**. The professor wrote up a detailed description of the person who bit the apple. The description said the person was tall and thin, and had high shoulders, large hands, large feet, a long narrow face, a fairly large nose, a protruding jaw, a distinctive **palate**, and crowded, overlapping teeth. Police found the fourth member of the unit after an anonymous tip-off, and he looked exactly the way the professor had described him.

Casts were made of the accused man's teeth. An independent **odontologist** found 16 points of similarity between the cast and the apple bite marks. This evidence, combined with the ballistics and other forensic evidence, was used to convict the man of the father and son murders and of being involved in the police murders.

Investigating the Investigators

Most forensic investigators are police members who have a science, engineering, or other relevant university degree. Outside experts are also involved. The following experts are just some of the experts involved in investigations that involve marks and imprints.

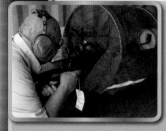

Ballistics Experts

Ballistics experts are specially trained people who examine firearms, bullets, cartridge cases, and other **projectiles**. They are often the same officers who examine weapons and tool marks.

Forensic Pathologists

Forensic pathologists are medical doctors who specialize in carrying out autopsies. Their main role is to discover how, when, and where a person died, but they also examine wounds on surviving victims. Pathologists often examine bloodstain patterns at the crime scene.

Crash Investigators

Crash investigators are also called major collision investigators. Crash investigators are trained in engineering, mechanics, or other related fields. They examine skid marks, crash debris, and crashed vehicles to discover the causes of road accidents.

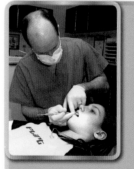

Orthodontists

Orthodontists are dentists who specialize in preventing and correcting teeth abnormalities and bite problems. They are the dentists a person goes to if they need braces. Orthodontists sometimes help out in forensic investigations.

Odontologists

Odontologists are dentists who study the structure, development, and any abnormalities of the teeth. These dentists are often used in forensic investigations, especially in bite mark examinations and to help identify bodies.

Glossary

abrasions	scratches or marks produced when two objects rub together
ante-mortem	before death
ballistics experts	experts who study firearms, bullets, cartridge cases, and projectiles
clotting factors	substances in the blood that help stop blood flow
databases	computer systems that hold data, such as fingerprints, that can be accessed by different people
forensic pathologists	medical doctors who specialize in carrying out autopsies
imperfections	faults
impression	mark, imprint, or print made by the pressure of an object on a surface
incident	violent, dangerous, or criminal event
macroscopic	visible to the eye without the need for a microscope
motive	reason for doing something
odontologist	dentist who studies the structure, development, and any abnormalities of the teeth
orthodontics	study of the prevention and correction of teeth abnormalities and bite problems
palate	roof of the mouth
pores	tiny openings in a surface
post-mortem	after death
projectiles	objects propelled through the air
striations	long parallel lines or ridges
tread	ridge and groove pattern on tires or the soles of shoes

Index